PEOPLE WHO . . .

By *wireless G*

RUNNING PRESS
PHILADELPHIA · LONDON

Published by Running Press,
A Member of the Perseus Books Group

Books published by Running Press are available at special discounts for bulk purchases in the United States by corporations, institutions, and other organizations. For more information, please contact the Special Markets Department at the Perseus Books Group, 2300 Chestnut Street, Suite 200, Philadelphia, PA 19103, or call (800) 810-4145, ext. 5000, or e-mail special.markets@perseusbooks.com.

ISBN 978-0-7624-4457-1
Library of Congress Control Number: 2011933255
E-book ISBN 978-0-7624-4498-4

9 8 7 6 5 4 3 2 1
Digit on the right indicates the number of this printing

Cover and interior design by Bill Jones
Illustrations by Jess Neil
Edited by Jordana Tusman
Typography: ITC Officina Serif and Helvetica Ultra Compressed

Running Press Book Publishers
2300 Chestnut Street
Philadelphia, PA 19103-4371

Visit us on the web!
www.runningpress.com

Foreword

By An Anonymous Academic
Whose Degrees Most Certainly
Do Not Come From
a For-Profit, Online University,
No Matter What You've Heard

"From whence came this lexicon of Peoples Who?" is a question I often hear intoned, and a fine question it is, for the matter of *wireless G* and his COMPREHENSIVE MANIFEST is a subject only the most full-bearded and bespectacled of scholars are privy to. Am I such a scholar, you ask? Your skepticism enrages me. It's true that my lost eyeball has forced me to settle for a bemonocled life, but such are the dangers of hunting the DEADLY NARWHAL.

Little is known of *wireless G*'s early life but that he was not always addressed as such! Indeed, his Christian name was *Wireford G. Galapagos III*. Born into wealth and privilege, young Wireford dreamed of the untethered life, hopping from network to network with naught but his aviator goggles and a deep, abiding disdain for his fellow man. Discarding his fortune and title, he ventured boldly into the wild bush of anthropological fieldwork, intent on observing and recording vivid descriptions of those people who confounded him with their CONTINUED, PERSISTENT EXISTENCE.

What you hold in your hands is his life's work: an ethnographic compendium of such astuteness, no one can escape its withering glare. Yet for all his well-documented vitriol toward those closest to him, *G* never impugns the People Who he has dedicated his life to pointing out. Nay, they are but described and assembled—printed and bound into this comprehensive volume. In it you will see your friends, your coworkers, and, if we are being perfectly frank, yourself. Mostly yourself.

Introduction

By *wireless G*

What can I say about myself that has not already been venomously mischaracterized by the scholar they got to write the foreword? And since when did a degree in refrigerator repair qualify one to conduct biographical scholarship? But let us endeavor to forget the childish musings of this anonymous degenerate, and focus instead on the resplendent volume you hold in your hands—and on me: its modest author. How could such a comprehensive compendium of peoples have been assembled by one man, you ask, even if that man was willing to offend all those who (once) loved him in the process? I know what you are thinking: *this compendium must have been the result of divine revelation, and* wireless G *is a modern-day prophet*. My answer? Perhaps!

But there were others (beyond the Abrahamic god) who helped as well: scurrilous roustabouts and high-tech dandiprats who spend more time dialing up the Inter'd-Webs than engaging in healthful pastimes like mustache waxing or hoop-and-stick. A sad affair, I can tell you, but these wiseacres have cyber-mailed me more than a little monkeyshine over the years, some of which demonstrated such genuine insight into the state of society that it supplements this very volume.

To them we all owe our heartfelt thanks, but it must be pointed out that the vast majority of (anthrax-free) mail I receive is filled instead with the most pedestrian of insights. Always eager to avoid reading, I turned to Rupert, my increasingly aggressive monkey butler. He, as it turns out, has as good an eye for identifying astute People Whos as myself. And by that I mean he is more accurately able to fling his feces at them. So nuanced a critic has he proven to be that, on a particularly furious night of editing, nary an inch of my offices (or my person) remained unsoiled by his steaming monkey pies. Oh, the times we've had!

I thusly invite you to peruse only the most thoroughly befouled of People Whos, compiled for the very first time in this anthropological compendium spanning the many varieties of man, and several varieties of woman as well.

PEOPLE WHO MAKE SURE YOU ARE AWARE THEY DON'T OWN A TELEVISION

PEOPLE WHO LOOK AT YOU WITH AN AIR OF STERN ANTICIPATION AS YOUR DOG FINISHES TAKING A SHIT

PEOPLE WHO SOMEHOW THINK IT'S OKAY TO REPEATEDLY CHECK THEIR PHONE, WHICH HAS THE RELATIVE BRIGHTNESS OF THE SUN, THROUGHOUT THE MOVIE

PEOPLE WHO GRUNT GRATUITOUSLY IN THE GYM

PEOPLE WHO SOMEHOW JUST NEVER SEEM TO HAVE FRIENDS OF THEIR OWN GENDER

PEOPLE WHO FORGET TO STAPLE THEIR PAPER, AND INSTEAD PERFORM AN ELABORATE BUT COMPLETELY INEFFECTUAL FORM OF ORIGAMI ON THE CORNER

PEOPLE WHO INTENTIONALLY MISSPELL THEIR CHILDREN'S NAMES UNDER THE GUISE OF CREATIVITY

PEOPLE WHO HAVE THEIR INFANT'S EARS PIERCED

PEOPLE WHO ARE WILLING TO WASTE A RAINFOREST'S WORTH OF PAPER TOWELS RATHER THAN TOUCH ANY SURFACE IN A PUBLIC RESTROOM

PEOPLE WHO DON'T EAT THE CRUSTS

PEOPLE WHO, AFTER YOU'VE UNFRIENDED THEM, SOMEHOW IMMEDIATELY KNOW IT WAS YOU AND SEND YOU A NEW FRIEND REQUEST

PEOPLE WHO USE EMAIL STATIONERY

PEOPLE WHO WATCH THEMSELVES IN THE STORE WINDOWS AS THEY WALK DOWN THE STREET

PEOPLE WHO GO FOR A NORMAL HIKE USING "TREKKING POLES"

PEOPLE WHO STAY UP ALL NIGHT COMMENTING IN ONLINE FORUMS TO RIDICULE PEOPLE WHO CAMPED OUT ALL NIGHT TO GET THE NEW IPHONE

PEOPLE WHO ARE WILLING TO TAKE THAT BALDNESS DRUG, WHICH CAUSES IMPOTENCE, IN ORDER TO ATTRACT WOMEN, TO HAVE SEX WITH

PEOPLE WHO BREATHE HEAVILY WHILE EATING

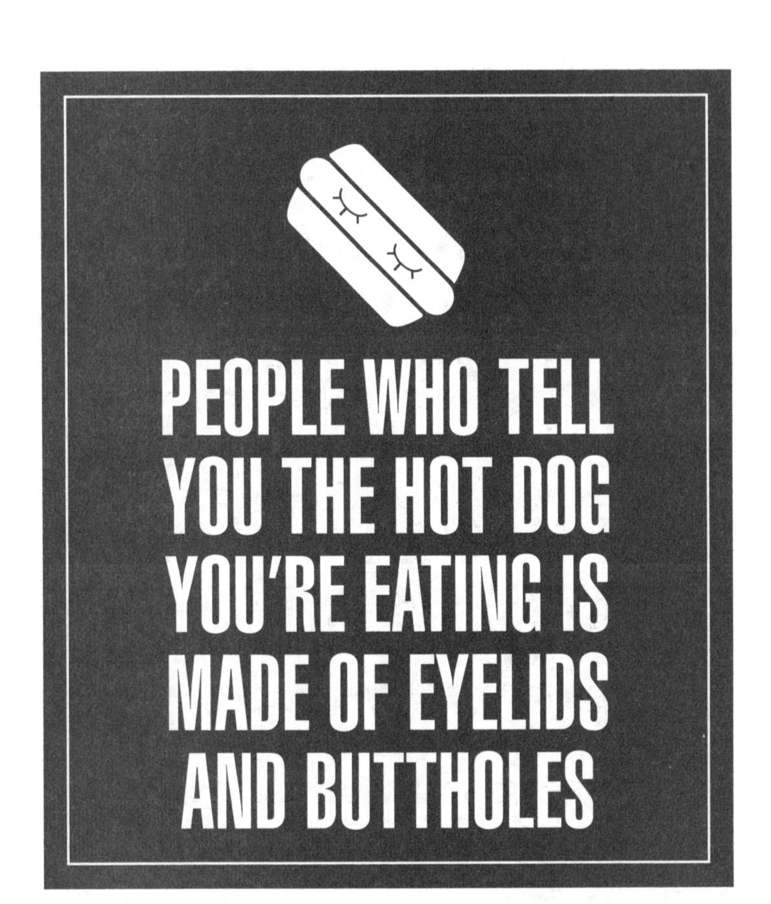
PEOPLE WHO TELL
YOU THE HOT DOG
YOU'RE EATING IS
MADE OF EYELIDS
AND BUTTHOLES

PEOPLE WHO WRITE "0" ON THE TIP LINE OF THEIR RECEIPTS, BECAUSE THEY'RE AFRAID IF THEY LEAVE IT BLANK SOMEONE WILL WRITE IN A TIP THEMSELVES

PEOPLE WHO VIGILANTLY MAINTAIN THE SEPARATION BETWEEN EACH TYPE OF FOOD ON THEIR PLATE

PEOPLE WHO ASK IF IT'S OKAY THAT THEY DATE YOUR EX

PEOPLE WHO DEACTIVATE THEIR FACEBOOK, MAKING YOU THINK THEY UNFRIENDED YOU, ONLY TO REAPPEAR A FEW WEEKS LATER

PEOPLE WHO CLEAN UP FOR THE MAID

PEOPLE WHO SAY "QUESTION!" BEFORE ASKING A QUESTION

PEOPLE WHO THINK AVOIDING COMIC SANS MAKES THEM A GRAPHIC DESIGNER

PEOPLE WHO SPEND THE WHOLE SHOW TRYING TO FILM THE BAND WITH THEIR PHONE

PEOPLE WHO ASK YOU TO IM THEM ON AOL INSTANT MESSENGER

PEOPLE WHO RESPOND "THAT'S WHAT SHE SAID" TO SOMETHING THAT THEY THEMSELVES HAVE SAID

PEOPLE WHO SHAVE THEIR PUBES, BUT NOT QUITE OFTEN ENOUGH

PEOPLE WHO JUST WON'T TAKE NO FOR AN ANSWER WHEN IT COMES TO BUTT SEX

PEOPLE WHO CAN ONLY PARALLEL PARK WHEN NO ONE IS THERE TO WATCH

PEOPLE WHO THINK A CAN OF FEBREZE PERFORMS MORE OR LESS THE SAME FUNCTION AS A WASHING MACHINE

PEOPLE WHO GO TO A SUSHI BAR AND GET THE TERIYAKI

PEOPLE WHO LOSE THEIR SHIT WHEN A GUY ISN'T CIRCUMCISED

PEOPLE WHO, WHEN ASKED WHETHER THEY WANT PAPER OR PLASTIC, NEED A MOMENT TO DECIDE

PEOPLE WHO LOOK OVER THEIR SPOUSE'S CREDIT CARD BILL AND ASSUME EVERY MEAL CHARGE IS EVIDENCE OF AN AFFAIR

PEOPLE WHO MOAN SOFTLY AS THEY BEGIN TO PEE

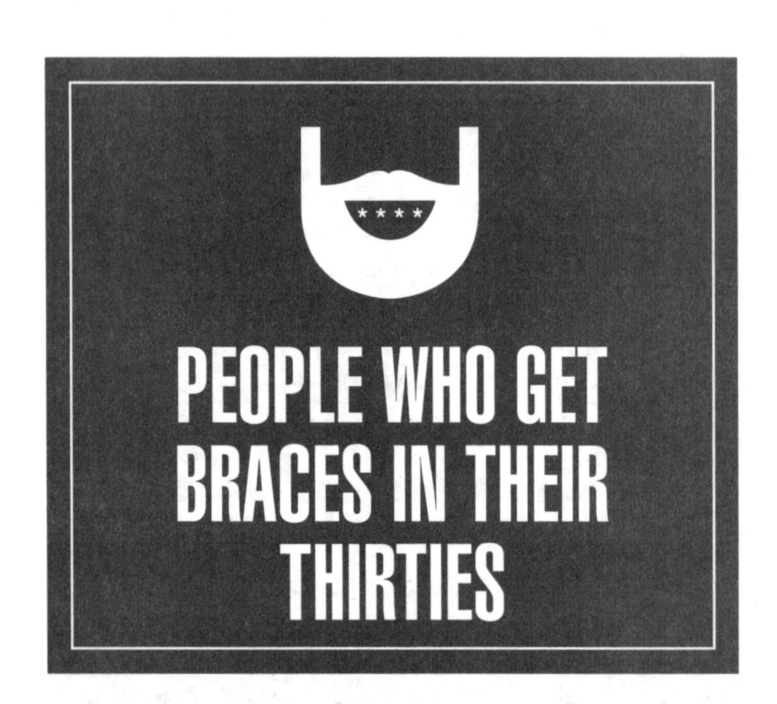

PEOPLE WHO WEAR THEIR BACKPACK ON THEIR FRONT

PEOPLE WHO SOMEHOW MANAGE TO KEEP EATING SOMETHING FOR, LIKE, THE ENTIRE MOVIE

PEOPLE WHO REFER TO CELEBRITIES BY THEIR FIRST NAMES

PEOPLE WHO PULL IN AHEAD OF YOU AT THE FAST FOOD DRIVE-THROUGH AND ORDER ENOUGH TO CATER A WEDDING BANQUET

PEOPLE WHO SAY THEIR PARENTS ARE THEIR BEST FRIENDS

PEOPLE WHO, WHEN YOU'RE WALKING TOWARD THEM IN A HALLWAY, GO LEFT INSTEAD OF RIGHT, FORCING YOU INTO A MOMENTARY SPASTIC DANCE

PEOPLE WHO APPARENTLY BELIEVE THE ONLY THING STANDING BETWEEN THEIR WRITING AND THAT OF DAVID SEDARIS IS INCREASED USE OF THE THESAURUS FUNCTION

PEOPLE WHO WON'T ACKNOWLEDGE THAT LIFTING THE TOILET SEAT REQUIRES THE SAME EFFORT AS PUTTING IT DOWN

PEOPLE WHO DESCRIBE THEMSELVES AS "HUMBLE"

PEOPLE WHO POST CLOSE-UP PICTURES OF THEMSELVES STARING OFF INTO THE DISTANCE AS THOUGH SOMEONE PHOTOGRAPHED THEM DURING A MOMENT OF PROFOUND INTROSPECTION, BUT WHICH ARE OBVIOUSLY SELF-PORTRAITS

PEOPLE W
ALONG WIT
THEY DON
THE WORDS TO

PEOPLE WHO RESPOND TO "HOW'S IT GOING?" WITH A GENUINE DESCRIPTION OF HOW IT IS, IN FACT, GOING

[illegible]EOPLE WHO, INSTEAD OF TRYING TO LEARN A BIT OF THE LANGUAGE OF THE COUNTRY THEY'RE VISITING, JUST SPEAK SLOWER AND LOUDER ENGLISH

PEOPLE WHO AGREE TO INSTALL THE TOOLBAR

PPL WHO CANT B BOTHRD 2 SPEL OWT TEH HOLE WORD OR PROFREED THEYRE POSTZ OR PUNK28 THERE SINTANZES OR RITE LEIK THAY PAASD 3ND GRAYD

PEOPLE WHO,
WHEN YOU TELL THEM
THEY HAVE FOOD ON
THEIR FACE, INSTEAD
OF USING A NAPKIN,
TRY TO GET IT WITH
THEIR TONGUE

PEOPLE WHO ATTACH AN ENORMOUS CUSTOM SPOILER TO THEIR TINY JAPANESE CAR

PEOPLE WHO LEAVE THE BATHROOM DOOR AJAR WHILE SHITTING

PEOPLE WHO THINK OTHERS WILL BE IMPRESSED THAT THEIR CAR MAKES MORE NOISE, RATHER THAN LESS

PEOPLE WHO THINK NICE CLOTHES ARE ONLY FOR WORK, SO THEY SHOW UP AT PARTIES IN DIRTY SWEATSHIRTS AND CARPENTER JEANS

PEOPLE WHO USE INTERNET EXPLORER

PEOPLE WHO THINK THE BEST WAY TO COMMUNICATE WITH GOD IS THROUGH THEIR FACEBOOK STATUS

PEOPLE WHO GO AHEAD AND TUCK THE T-SHIRT INTO THEIR BELTED SHORTS

PEOPLE WHO LISTEN TO VIDEO GAME SOUNDTRACKS WHEN THEY'RE NOT PLAYING VIDEO GAMES

PEOPLE WHO GIVE YOU A PRESENT IN A GIFT BAG, AND THEN ASK FOR THE BAG BACK

PEOPLE WHO, WHEN YOU BRING UP THE POSSIBILITY OF GETTING SOME COSMETIC SURGERY, MAKE NO EFFORT TO TALK YOU OUT OF IT

PEOPLE WHO LEAVE VOICEMAILS

PEOPLE WHO TAKE PRIDE IN HOW INFREQUENTLY THEY NEED TO PEE

PEOPLE WHOSE ONLINE DATING PROFILE USES THE PHRASE "PARTNER IN CRIME"

PEOPLE WHO SAVE FORTUNE COOKIE FORTUNES

PEOPLE WHO ARE SO SLOW WALKING DOWN THE STREET THAT YOU ABSOLUTELY MUST PASS THEM BUT SO FAT THAT YOU CAN'T

PEOPLE WHO USE BRITISH SPELLINGS AND PRETEND THEY DIDN'T REALISE

PEOPLE WHO IMPLY THEY ARE SOMEHOW MEDICALLY PROHIBITED FROM WEARING A CONDOM

PEOPLE WHO SING THE GUITAR SOLO

PEOPLE WHO ARE RELUCTANT TO GET A SMARTPHONE BECAUSE THEY SPENT SO MUCH TIME LEARNING TO TEXT ON A KEYPAD

PEOPLE WHO THINK THE ONLY REASON ANYONE BUYS NON-APPLE COMPUTERS IS BECAUSE THEY'RE POOR

PEOPLE WHO TILE DESKTOP IMAGES THAT AREN'T PATTERNS

PEOPLE WHO SPEND HOURS ONLINE MAKING WRY OBSERVATIONS ABOUT THE ABSURDITY OF HIPSTERS, BUT WHO ARE OBVIOUSLY HIPSTERS THEMSELVES

PEOPLE WHO, WHEN TOURING A CITY THAT ISN'T LONDON, NEVERTHELESS MANAGE TO DO IT FROM A RED DOUBLE-DECKER BUS

PEOPLE WHO ARE STILL TALKING ABOUT CARBS

PEOPLE WHO THINK YOU PAID THE $10 ADMISSION TO LISTEN TO THEIR OPINIONS OF THE FILM

PEOPLE WHO THINK HALLOWEEN CELEBRATES DRESSING LIKE A WHORE

PEOPLE WHO LEAVE THEIR NEUROTIC DOGS IN THE CAR, MAKING YOUR WALK THROUGH THE PARKING LOT LIKE NAVIGATING A HOUSE OF HORRORS

PEOPLE WHO FLOSS IN THE LIVING ROOM

PEOPLE WHO, WHEN YOU START TALKING TO THEM, INSTEAD OF TAKING OFF THEIR HEADPHONES, JUST POINT TO THEM AND SHRUG

PEOPLE WHO ORDER CHEESE PIZZA

PEOPLE WHO APPLAUD WHEN THE PLANE LANDS

PEOPLE WHO GET ON AN EARLY MORNING FLIGHT AND IMMEDIATELY START IN WITH THE BLOODY MARYS

PEOPLE WHO MAKE EXCESSIVE EYE CONTACT AND REPEAT YOUR NAME A LOT, AS THOUGH THEY LEARNED SOCIALIZATION FROM A BUSINESS NETWORKING BOOK IN THE AIRPORT

PEOPLE WHO CLAIM THEY HAVE NO IDEA YOU AREN'T SUPPOSED TO FLUSH THE TOILET WHILE SOMEONE IS IN THE SHOWER

PEOPLE WHO NEED A DONGLE TO CONNECT

PEOPLE WHO
JUST KEEP LISTENING
TO THE SAME BANDS
THEY LIKED IN COLLEGE
FOR THE REST OF
THEIR LIVES

PEOPLE WHO, DESPITE
HAVING A PENIS, SIT
DOWN TO PEE

PEOPLE WHO FIND A WAY TO LET YOU KNOW HOW FREQUENTLY THEY WORK OUT

PEOPLE WHO ANNOUNCE THE RESULTS OF THEIR LAVATORY VISIT TO THE ROOM

PEOPLE WHO CANNOT IDENTIFY A CLEAR LINE BETWEEN WHAT THEY WEAR AS PAJAMAS AND THE REST OF THEIR CLOTHING

PEOPLE WHO STILL GO OUT AND BUY THE CD

PEOPLE WHO STORE SMALL OBJECTS IN THEIR CLEAVAGE

PEOPLE WHO CLAIM TO BE VEGETARIAN, "EXCEPT FOR BACON"

PEOPLE WHO REASSURE YOU THAT THEY AGREE PSYCHICS ARE FULL OF SHIT, BUT STILL WANT TO TELL YOU ALL ABOUT WHAT THE PSYCHIC SAID, AND DO YOU THINK THERE MIGHT BE SOMETHING TO IT?

PEOPLE WHO ARE STILL SUPPORTED BY THEIR PARENTS, BUT SOMEHOW ALSO COLLECT UNEMPLOYMENT

PEOPLE WHO STOP UNEXPECTEDLY IN DOORWAYS

PEOPLE WHO WON'T GIVE YOU ANYTHING FOR FREE WHEN YOU SHOW UP AT THE STORE THEY WORK IN, BECAUSE THEY THINK THERE'S A CAMERA SOMEWHERE

PEOPLE WHO SIT THERE AT FOUR-WAY STOP SIGNS AS YOU DRIVE UP, WAITING FOR YOU TO COME TO A FULL STOP BEFORE THEY FINALLY MAKE THEIR TURN, JUST IN CASE

PEOPLE WHO REFUSE TO YIELD THE ARMREST, EVEN THOUGH YOU'RE STUCK IN THE MIDDLE SEAT AND THEY HAVE NO COMPETITION FOR THEIR OTHER ONE

PEOPLE WHO, AFTER SHAKING YOUR HAND, CAN'T EVEN WAIT UNTIL YOU'RE NOT LOOKING TO WIPE THEIRS OFF ON THEIR PANTS

PEOPLE WHO WORK AT THE RENAISSANCE FAIR AND HAVE ABSOLUTELY NO ABILITY TO DO AN ENGLISH ACCENT, BUT WHO SOMEHOW THINK RELENTLESS EFFORT WILL MAKE UP FOR IT. ACTUALLY. . . JUST ANYONE WHO WORKS AT THE RENAISSANCE FAIR

PEOPLE WHO THINK THEY CAN SINGLE-HANDEDLY CORRECT THE GRAMMAR OF THE INTERNET

PEOPLE WHO, AFTER THE LIGHT TURNS GREEN, JUST CONTINUE HAMMERING OUT THEIR TEXT MESSAGE

PEOPLE WHO EAT STRING CHEESE INCORRECTLY

PEOPLE WHO GIVE AN ONGOING PLAY-BY-PLAY DURING THEIR SEXUAL ENCOUNTERS

PEOPLE WHO PRETEND NOT TO REALIZE HOW POWERFULLY THEIR APARTMENT SMELLS OF CAT PISS

PEOPLE WHO CAN'T COME TO GRIPS WITH THE FACT THAT THEY'VE REACHED THE AGE AT WHICH NOSE-HAIR TRIMMING IS NO LONGER OPTIONAL

PEOPLE WHO WON'T START DRIVING AGAIN UNTIL THE PEDESTRIAN HAS NOT ONLY CLEARED THE CROSSWALK, BUT HAS ESSENTIALLY PASSED THE HORIZON LINE

PEOPLE WHO WALK UP TO YOU AT THE GYM AND TELL YOU, UNPROMPTED, THAT YOU'RE DOING IT WRONG

PEOPLE WHO STILL CHECK THEIR MYSPACE

PEOPLE WHO JUST ASSUME YOU DON'T WANT TO SEE THE DESSERT MENU

PEOPLE WHO SEEMINGLY HAVE NO AWARENESS OF MOVING-WALKWAY ETIQUETTE

PEOPLE WHO THINK THE WAY TO GET THEIR EX BACK IS TO KEEP CALLING YOU FOR ONE MORE ROUND OF POST-RELATIONSHIP ANALYSIS

@PEOPLEWHO USE THE "@" SYMBOL TO INDICATE WHOM THEY'RE ADDRESSING, EVEN WHEN THEY'RE NOT ON TWITTER AND IT THEREFORE SERVES NO PURPOSE

PEOPLE WHO CITE YOUR NOT HAVING LOGGED OUT AS JUSTIFICATION FOR GOING THROUGH YOUR EMAIL

PEOPLE WHO TELL YOU HOW HOT THEIR COUSIN IS

PEOPLE WHO GO THE SPEED LIMIT IN THE FAST LANE

PEOPLE WHO THINK EVERY SOCIAL NETWORK IS JUST ANOTHER PLACE TO PUBLISH THEIR ASININE TWITTER FEED

PEOPLE WHO GREET YOU WITH A CONFIDENT "NICE TO MEET YOU!" THOUGH YOU'VE MET THEM SEVERAL TIMES BEFORE

PEOPLE WHO POST UPDATES CONGRATULATING EVERYONE FOR HAVING SURVIVED THEIR FACEBOOK FRIEND PURGE

PEOPLE WHO NERVOUSLY PUMP THEIR LEG UP AND DOWN UNDER THE TABLE

PEOPLE WHO WEAR WOOL CAPS IN THE SUMMER

PEOPLE WHO GIVE OUT BOXES OF RAISINS ON HALLOWEEN

PEOPLE WHO SPEND THE WHOLE SHOWER WASHING YOUR BOOBS

PEOPLE WHO, THE MOMENT THEY SLEEP WITH SOMEONE NEW, MAKE SURE THEIR EX FINDS OUT ABOUT IT

PEOPLE WHO INSIST ON BUYING THE MOST EXPENSIVE DOG FOOD, THOUGH THEIR DOG WOULD, GIVEN THE OPPORTUNITY, RATHER EAT ITS OWN SHIT

PEOPLE WHO WON'T ACCEPT THAT THEY CAN EAT VEGETABLES AT A NORMAL RESTAURANT, BUT YOU CAN'T EAT MEAT AT A VEGETARIAN RESTAURANT

PEOPLE WHO "SIGN" DOCUMENTS WITH A CURSIVE FONT

PEOPLE WHO ASK YOU TO KEEP THEIR PHONE IN YOUR BAG, BUT THEN WANT TO CHECK IT EVERY FIVE MINUTES

PEOPLE WHO CLAIM EVERY AWFUL REALITY SHOW THEY WATCH IS A "GUILTY PLEASURE," BUT NEVER SEEM TO FEEL QUITE GUILTY ENOUGH TO JUST STOP WATCHING AWFUL REALITY SHOWS

PEOPLE WHO USE THE HANDICAPPED ENTRY BUTTON BECAUSE THEY FEAR DOORKNOB GERMS

PEOPLE WHO HAVE STRONG OPINIONS ABOUT CELL PHONE OPERATING SYSTEMS

PEOPLE WHO SPENT A SEMESTER ABROAD YEARS AGO, BUT STILL MANAGE TO WORK IT INTO MOST CONVERSATIONS

PEOPLE WHO GIVE THEIR PETS HUMAN NAMES

PEOPLE WHO START A CONVERSATION IN THE ELEVATOR MOMENTS BEFORE IT ARRIVES ON YOUR FLOOR, GIVING YOU ALMOST NO TIME TO SHIFT FROM FEIGNING INTEREST TO FEIGNING DISAPPOINTMENT

PEOPLE WHO THINK A GOOD WAY TO ESTABLISH A DISTINCT IDENTITY FOR THEMSELVES IS THROUGH NOVELTY FACIAL HAIR

PEOPLE WHO, UNDETERRED BY COURTESY OR SOCIAL DECORUM, NEVER TURN OFF THE TV

PEOPLE WHO DO STRETCHES IN PUBLIC

PEOPLE WHO JUST UNILATERALLY DECIDE THEY'RE TAKING A SIP FROM EVERYONE'S DRINK

PEOPLE WHO HESITATE NOTICEABLY BEFORE STEPPING ON THE ESCALATOR people who capitalize whichever Random Words they want To emphasize

PEOPLE WHOSE EXTENSIVE TATTOO WORK AMOUNTS TO A SCATTER CHART OF FAILED RELATIONSHIPS

PEOPLE WHO THINK PRESSING ELEVATOR BUTTONS REPEATEDLY MAKES THE ELEVATOR GO FASTER

PEOPLE WHO HAVE AN UMBRELLA BUT WALK UNDER THE AWNING ANYWAY

PEOPLE WHO, WHEN GOING OUT TO THE MOVIES, LEAVE AN EMPTY SEAT BETWEEN THEMSELVES AND THEIR BUDDY TO PROVE HETEROSEXUALITY

PEOPLE WHO STILL "KICK IT, OLD-SCHOOL"

PEOPLE WHO THINK ORAL SEX IS DISGUSTING, UNLESS IT'S BEING PERFORMED ON THEM

PEOPLE WHO ASSERT THAT DOLPHINS ARE, IN A WAY, SMARTER THAN HUMANS

PEOPLE WHO BEMOAN THEIR LOST YOUTH WHEN TURNING TWENTY-FIVE

PEOPLE WHO LET YOU GO THROUGH THE WHOLE DAY WITHOUT POINTING OUT THAT YOUR FLY IS OPEN

PEOPLE WHO INSIST YOU SHOULDN'T PUT Q-TIPS IN YOUR EARS

PEOPLE WHO HAVE MORE DEVICES CONNECTED TO THEIR TV THAN THEY HAVE FRIENDS TO COME OVER AND WATCH IT

PEOPLE WHO TOOK ONE PSYCH CLASS IN COLLEGE BUT NEVER MISS A CHANCE TO VOLUNTEER A DIAGNOSIS

PEOPLE WHO BLOW THEIR NOSE AT THE TABLE

PEOPLE WHO THINK AROMATHERAPY CANDLES ARE A GOOD SUBSTITUTE FOR CLEANING OUT THEIR TURD-FILLED CAT LITTER BOX

PEOPLE WHO BRING A BOTTLE OF WINE TO YOUR HOUSE, AND THEN TAKE IT WITH THEM WHEN THEY LEAVE

PEOPLE WHO ARE STILL WAITING TO SEE IF THIS WHOLE "TEXTING" THING IS WORTHWHILE

PEOPLE WHO TELL YOU ABOUT THEIR GENITAL SHAVING MISHAPS

"PEOPLE" WHO CONSTANTLY MAKE "AIR QUOTES"

PEOPLE WHO GO ON THE INTERACTIVE AUDIO TOUR

PEOPLE WHO THINK HOVERING NEARBY WILL MAKE YOU MORE LIKELY TO BUY SOMETHING FROM THEIR STORE

PEOPLE WHO ASK THE WAITRESS IF THEY HAVE SPLENDA

PEOPLE WHO WON'T STOP COMPLAINING TO YOU ABOUT HOW FAT THEY ARE, DESPITE THE FACT THAT YOU ARE VISIBLY FATTER THAN THEM

PEOPLE WHO TELL YOU THAT YOU LOOK TIRED

PEOPLE WHO SEEM WILLFULLY UNAWARE OF ALL THE DIRTY LOOKS THEY'RE GETTING FOR HAVING THEIR CHILD ON A LEASH

PEOPLE WHO DON'T KNOW THE DIFFERENCE BETWEEN ITS AND IT'S, BUT SOMEHOW THINK ITS' IS A WORD

PEOPLE WHO STILL WEAR A WATCH

PEOPLE WHO CREATE FACEBOOK PROFILES FOR THEIR PETS

PEOPLE WHO MAKE UP FOR NEVER HAVING SEX THEMSELVES BY FORCING THEIR SIMS TO FUCK LIKE RABBITS

PEOPLE WHO MISTAKE LAURENCE FISHBURNE FOR SAMUEL L. JACKSON

PEOPLE WITH MULTIPLE, CONTRADICTORY REASONS FOR BEING VEGETARIAN

PEOPLE WHO BUILD UP A MOVIE QUOTE SO MUCH THAT, WHEN YOU FINALLY SEE THE FILM, THE RELEVANT SCENE IS SADLY UNDERWHELMING

PEOPLE WHO CAN'T GET PAST SOMEONE NOT WANTING TO SMOKE THEIR DOPE

PEOPLE WHO SPEND FORTY-FIVE MINUTES BEFOULING THE PLANE'S ONLY BATHROOM

PEOPLE WHO CALL
IT "GUYLINER" AS
THOUGH THAT
EXPLAINS WHY
THEY'RE A GUY WHO'S
WEARING EYELINER

PEOPLE WHO GO TO BARS ALONE AND JUST FIDDLE WITH THEIR PHONE WHILE HOPING SOMEONE WILL TALK TO THEM

PEOPLE WHO ONLY READ WHILE SHITTING

PEOPLE WHO, OUT OF THE BLUE, DECIDE THEY ARE ALLERGIC TO GLUTEN

PEOPLE WHO LEAVE HALF THE YOGURT ON THE SPOON WHEN THEY PULL IT OUT OF THEIR MOUTH

PEOPLE WHO SPRINT FOR THE BATHROOM IMMEDIATELY AFTER SEX

PEOPLE WHO READ THE NUTRITIONAL INFORMATION AT THE DRIVE-THROUGH

PEOPLE WHO, WHEN YOU'RE TALKING TO THEM DIRECTLY IN A FACE-TO-FACE CONVERSATION, START CHECKING THEIR PHONE

PEOPLE WHO "LIKE" ALL YOUR OLD PROFILE PICTURES AT THREE IN THE MORNING

PEOPLE WHO SHOW UP AT THE AIRPORT WEARING, ESSENTIALLY, PAJAMAS

PEOPLE WHO DON'T UN-RECLINE THEIR SEAT DURING THE MEAL SERVICE

PEOPLE WHO SHUSH YOU DURING THE COMMERCIALS BEFORE THE MOVIE

PEOPLE WHO PRODUCE VIOLENT, AUDIBLE BOWEL MOVEMENTS IN PUBLIC RESTROOMS

PEOPLE WHO WON'T GO WHEN IT'S THEIR TURN AT A FOUR-WAY INTERSECTION

PEOPLE WHO TRY TO PASS OFF STUFF THEY HEARD ON NPR AS THEIR OWN INSIGHTS

PEOPLE WHO CAN ONLY OPEN UP TO ANONYMOUS STRANGERS ONLINE

PEOPLE WHO LOOK AS IF THEY'RE GOING TO SAY "HI" AS THEY PASS YOU, CAUSING YOU TO SAY "HI" TO THEM, BUT THEN THEY JUST KEEP WALKING

PEOPLE WHO HAVE A THEME WEDDING

PEOPLE WHO MARRY THE FIRST PERSON THEY HAVE SEX WITH

PEOPLE WHOSE DIET HAS NOT CHANGED SINCE ELEMENTARY SCHOOL

PEOPLE WHO INSIST THE *HARRY POTTER* BOOKS AREN'T FOR CHILDREN

PEOPLE WHO LISTEN TO THE DIRECTOR'S COMMENTARY

PEOPLE WHO DEBATE POLITICS IN THE COMMENTS SECTION OF YOUTUBE VIDEOS

PEOPLE WHO START EATING WHILE THEY'RE STILL GOING THROUGH THE BUFFET

PEOPLE WHO WEAR SHOES THAT SEPARATE EACH TOE

PEOPLE WHO ASK THE WAITRESS FOLLOW-UP QUESTIONS

PEOPLE WHO REFER TO THEMSELVES AS THEIR CAT'S "MOMMY"

PEOPLE WHO CAN'T SEEM TO GET IT THROUGH THEIR HEAD THAT YOU LIVE IN A DIFFERENT FUCKING TIME ZONE

PEOPLE WHO, WHEN CALCULATING THEIR SHARE, MYSTERIOUSLY FORGET ABOUT TAX AND TIP

PEOPLE WHO PUT STEREO SPEAKERS RIGHT NEXT TO EACH OTHER

PEOPLE WHO TAKE A PHOTO OF A FLOWER WITH A BLURRY BACKGROUND AND IMMEDIATELY DESCRIBE THEMSELVES AS AN "ASPIRING PHOTOGRAPHER"

PEOPLE WHO DON'T LET THE FACT THAT THEY ONLY EVER LEARNED THREE CHORDS ON THE GUITAR PREVENT THEM FROM CONSTANTLY PLAYING SAID GUITAR

PEOPLE WHO THINK BLOCKING THEIR PHONE NUMBER FROM CALLER ID WILL MAKE YOU SUDDENLY WANT TO TALK TO THEM AGAIN

PEOPLE WHO WON'T SING IN THE CAR

PEOPLE WHO KEEP TABS ON WHAT CELEBRITIES' CHILDREN ARE WEARING

PEOPLE WHO USE THE PHRASE "ACTION ITEMS" OUTSIDE OF WORK

PEOPLE WHO, WHILE DRIVING IN FRONT OF YOU, SLOW ALMOST TO A COMPLETE STOP BEFORE TAKING A RIGHT TURN

PEOPLE WHO "LIKE" THEIR OWN POSTS ON FACEBOOK

PEOPLE WHO DESCRIBE THEMSELVES AS WORLD TRAVELERS, BUT DON'T SEEM TO HAVE NOTICED THERE ARE PLACES IN THE WORLD THAT AREN'T EUROPE

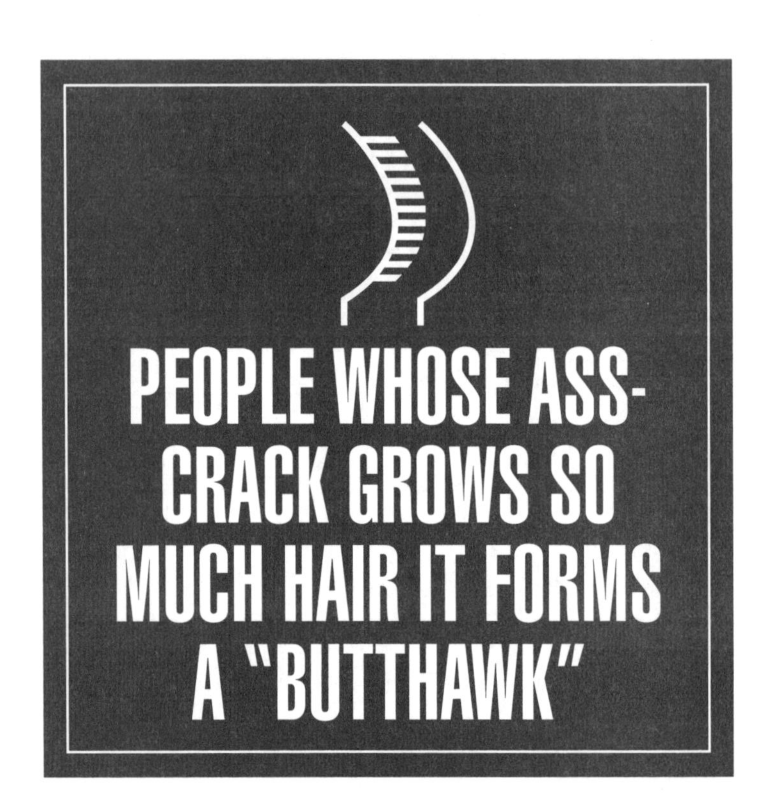

PEOPLE WHO WON'T SHUT UP ABOUT YOGA

PEOPLE WHO ASK THE PROFESSOR QUESTIONS ABOUT THE EXAM THAT ARE ANSWERED IN THE STUDY GUIDE THAT THE PROFESSOR JUST HANDED THEM

PEOPLE WHOSE PROFILE PICTURE IS OBVIOUSLY INTENDED TO PREVENT SNOOPING EXES FROM DISCOVERING HOW MONSTROUSLY FAT THEY'VE BECOME

PEOPLE WHO THINK LEARNING THE DIFFERENCE BETWEEN "YOUR" AND "YOU'RE" IS A PROJECT THAT CAN ALWAYS WAIT UNTIL NEXT YEAR

PEOPLE WHO REFER TO CALIFORNIA AS "CALI"

PEOPLE WHO MAKE A FACTUAL CLAIM WHICH, WHEN LATER DISPROVED, THEY CONTINUE TO INSIST IS TRUE, AND IT'S THE ENTIRE INTERNET THAT HAS IT WRONG

PEOPLE WHO PRETEND TO RECOGNIZE OBSCURE AUTHORS

PEOPLE WHO TALK ABOUT CHARACTERS ON TV SHOWS AS THOUGH THEY WERE ACTUAL PEOPLE

PEOPLE WHO CALL YOU ONLY BECAUSE THEY'RE BORED WHEN DRIVING SOMEWHERE, AND THEN END THE CONVERSATION ABRUPTLY WHEN THEY ARRIVE

PEOPLE WHO PAT DOWN THEIR PIZZA WITH NAPKINS

PEOPLE WHO THINK A SLOWLY RUNNING FAUCET WILL IN ANY WAY OBSCURE THE DEAFENING TUMULT OF THEIR SHIT-MAKING

PEOPLE WHOSE LOVEMAKING TECHNIQUES CLEARLY ALL ORIGINATED IN A CHILDHOOD RIFE WITH INTERNET PORN

PEOPLE WHO REFER TO THEIR PENIS IN THE THIRD PERSON

PEOPLE WHO INSIST ON USING SEMICOLONS DESPITE HAVING NO; IDEA WHERE THEY GO

PEOPLE WHO ASK FOR FORTUNE COOKIES AT THAI RESTAURANTS

PEOPLE WHO DON'T PRONOUNCE THE "H" IN "HUMID"

PEOPLE WHO THROW HALF THEIR DINNER IN YOUR SINK BECAUSE THEY JUST ASSUME YOU'VE GOT A GARBAGE DISPOSAL

PEOPLE WHO YOU OBVIOUSLY HAVE A CRUSH ON, BUT WHO ASK YOU TO HELP THEM GET TOGETHER WITH YOUR FRIEND

PEOPLE WHO INSIST THEIR CAT "THINKS HE'S A DOG"

PEOPLE WHO GLARE RESENTFULLY WHEN NO ONE SAYS "BLESS YOU" AFTER THEY'VE SNEEZED

PEOPLE WHO REGARD "ALL YOU CAN EAT" AS A PERSONAL CHALLENGE

PEOPLE WHO ARE IN FIRST CLASS WHEN YOU ARE NOT

PEOPLE WHO GET TATTOOS OF WORDS IN LANGUAGES THEY DON'T UNDERSTAND

PEOPLE WHO WALK INTO THE MEETING LATE AND THEN ASK ABOUT ALL THE THINGS YOU JUST DISCUSSED

PEOPLE WHO ASK YOU TO HELP THEM MOVE, BUT HAVEN'T DONE ANY PACKING BY THE TIME YOU SHOW UP

PEOPLE WHOSE ADDICTION TO SUNSCREEN BORDERS ON THE VAMPIRIC

PEOPLE WHO POST UPDATES QUOTING THEIR OWN CHILD, WHO IS NEITHER FUNNY NOR INTERESTING TO ANYONE ELSE

PEOPLE WHO STILL QUOTE *OFFICE SPACE*

PEOPLE WHO, AFTER YOU SEND THEM A TEXT MESSAGE, IMMEDIATELY CALL YOU ON THE PHONE

PEOPLE WHO BELIEVE THAT VIRGINITY AND BLOW JOBS CAN COEXIST PEACEFULLY

PEOPLE WHO GO ON VACATION AND COMPLAIN ABOUT THE TOURISTS

PEOPLE WHO INSIST VINYL ACTUALLY SOUNDS BETTER

PEOPLE WHO APPLY A "RETRO" FILTER TO EVERY SINGLE PHOTO

PEOPLE WHO DISCOVER NEW BANDS ONLY WHEN THEY'RE INTERVIEWED ON NPR

PEOPLE WHO ARE ON "TEAM JACOB" OR "TEAM EDWARD"

PEOPLE WHO TAG THEMSELVES IN THEIR OWN PROFILE PICTURES

PEOPLE WHO THINK WEARING WOMEN'S JEANS WILL ATTRACT WOMEN TO THEM

PEOPLE WHO PUT ON MAKEUP TO GO TO THE GYM

PEOPLE WHO REFER TO THEIR BREASTS AS "THE GIRLS"

PEOPLE WHO WRITE THEIR WHOLE EMAIL IN THE SUBJECT LINE

PEOPLE WHO STILL USE BOOLEAN OPERATORS WHEN GOOGLING *AND* YAHOOING *OR* BINGING

PEOPLE WHO AVOID THE RED M&Ms

PEOPLE WHO INSIST THAT THE MUSIC SCENE WAS SO MUCH BETTER IN AN ERA THAT THEY WERE NOT EVEN ALIVE TO EXPERIENCE

PEOPLE WHO INSIST ON UNWRAPPING GIFTS IN SUCH A WAY AS TO CAUSE ABSOLUTELY NO DAMAGE TO THE WRAPPING PAPER

PEOPLE WHO CLAIM THEY "FORGET TO EAT"

PEOPLE WHO START TYPING SOMETHING IN CHAT, BUT THEN AFTER A WHILE THE INDICATOR GOES OFF, AND THEY NEVER ACTUALLY SEND ANYTHING

PEOPLE WHO ACCOMPLISH THINGS AND THEN TELL YOU ABOUT THEM, KNOWING FULL WELL YOU'VE NEVER DONE SHIT

PEOPLE WHO PRETEND TO HATE THAT THEIR POSSESSIVE BOYFRIEND HARASSES ANY GUY WHO TALKS TO THEM, BUT IN FACT THAT'S THE ONLY THING KEEPING THEM TOGETHER

PEOPLE WHO WON'T LET ANYONE FLIP CHANNELS DURING THE COMMERCIALS, BECAUSE THEY "DON'T WANT TO MISS ANYTHING"

PEOPLE WHO FEEL THEIR WEBSITE NEEDS AN ELABORATE FLASH INTRO, THE LOADING TIME FOR WHICH IS LONGER THAN ANYONE HAD PLANNED TO SPEND ON THE SITE AS A WHOLE

PEOPLE WHO HEARD I WAS A VERY RELIABLE PERSON (GOD BE PRAISED) THROUGH WHOM TO FUNNEL THE 500 MILLION DOLLARS THAT THEIR DEAD UNCLE, A WEALTHY BANKER FROM NIGERIA, IS HAVING TROUBLE GETTING OUT OF THE COUNTRY

PEOPLE WHO ARE PRETTY SURE THAT EXAGGERATING THEIR HEIGHT BY FIVE INCHES ON MATCH.COM IS A SOLID LONG-TERM DATING STRATEGY

PEOPLE WHO COULD EASILY SOLVE THEIR PERPETUAL MUFFIN TOP IF THEY'D JUST BUY THE GIANT PANTS THEY NEED

PEOPLE WHO MAKE A CALL THE MOMENT THE PLANE LANDS

PEOPLE WHO THINK HITTING REFRESH REPEATEDLY WILL MAKE THE WEB PAGE LOAD FASTER

PEOPLE WHO USE A CELL PHONE HOLSTER

PEOPLE WHO DON'T
LET MALE PATTERN
BALDNESS STOP THEM
FROM MAINTAINING
THAT EPIC PONYTAIL

PEOPLE WHO FIND A WAY TO MAKE SURE THE MEETING FILLS ITS FULL ALLOTTED TIME

PEOPLE WHO MAKE IT A POINT OF PRIDE THAT THE ONLY NEWS THEY GET IS FROM *THE DAILY SHOW*

PEOPLE WHO, IN THE MIDDLE OF A SONG, BREAK INTO SPONTANEOUS "AIR DRUMMING"

PEOPLE WHO LOUDLY ANNOUNCE IT WHEN THEY'RE ABOUT TO HAVE AN ORGASM

PEOPLE WHO TAKE THEIR FOOD OUT OF THE MICROWAVE BEFORE THE TIME IS UP, BUT DON'T HIT "RESET"

PEOPLE WHO EAT SALAD WITHOUT DRESSING

PEOPLE WHO TAKE DOWN THEIR CHRISTMAS DECORATIONS ON CHRISTMAS

PEOPLE WHO WONDER ALOUD IF THE PERSON THEY'RE DATING IS THEIR "SOULMATE"

PEOPLE WHO ARRANGE ALL THEIR DOLLAR BILLS NEATLY IN THEIR WALLET, PUT THE WALLET CAREFULLY IN THEIR BAG, AND ZIP UP THEIR JACKET BEFORE RELUCTANTLY LEAVING THE GROCERY CHECK-OUT LINE

PEOPLE WHO FEEL THEIR PURSE IS MORE DESERVING OF A SEAT THAN THE SEATLESS HUMANS HOVERING NEARBY

PEOPLE WHO KEEP THEIR SOCKS ON DURING SEX

PEOPLE WHO THINK THEY CAN GET AWAY WITH HAVING SEX WHILE YOU'RE IN THE ROOM, IF THEY'RE "REALLY QUIET"

PEOPLE WHO MISTAKE YOUR SILENCE FOR APPROVAL

PEOPLE WHO ARE ONLY ABLE TO EXPRESS EMOTIONS THROUGH EMOTICONS

PEOPLE WHO DRESS LIKE THEY'RE OUT CLUBBING, BUT IT'S THE MIDDLE OF THE DAY

PEOPLE WHOSE DOG FITS IN THEIR PURSE

PEOPLE WHO MAKE MAJOR ELECTRONICS PURCHASES AT THE AIRPORT

PEOPLE WHO HAVE WORDS PRINTED ACROSS THE ASS OF THEIR SWEATPANTS

PEOPLE WHO TRY TO GET ON THE ELEVATOR BEFORE YOU CAN GET OUT

PEOPLE WHO MAKE IT IMPOSSIBLE TO IGNORE THEIR GUM CHEWING

PEOPLE WHO TRY TO PUSH PAST YOU AT THE CONCERT BECAUSE THEY "HAVE SOME FRIENDS DOWN FRONT"

PEOPLE WHO CHUCKLE CONDESCENDINGLY WHEN YOU TELL THEM A BAND YOU LIKE

PEOPLE WHO COME OUT OF THE BATHROOM HAVING COMPLETED AN ENTIRE LEVEL OF ANGRY BIRDS

PEOPLE WHO NEVER SEEM TO WEAR A STITCH OF CLOTHING FROM THE MOMENT THEY ENTER THE LOCKER ROOM

PEOPLE WHO TRY TO TEXT WHILE ON THE DANCE FLOOR

PEOPLE WHO TEXT GUYS PHOTOS OF THEIR TITS AND DON'T EXPECT THEM TO SHOW UP ONLINE

PEOPLE WHO LISTEN TO CASSETTE TAPES FOR THE HIPSTER IRONY

PEOPLE WHO LEAVE SPACES IN FRONT OF PERIODS .

PEOPLE WHO GET UNCOMFORTABLY ANGRY WITH THEIR BOARD GAME TEAMMATE

PEOPLE WHOSE BLOG ENTRIES ARE LONGER THAN ONE SENTENCE

PEOPLE WHO HAVE FURNITURE EXPLICITLY DESIGNED TO DISPLAY THEIR CD COLLECTION

PEOPLE WHO DON'T TELL YOU WHEN THERE'S SAUCE ON YOUR FACE

PEOPLE WHO HAVE ALREADY BOUGHT THEIR THANKSGIVING PLANE TICKETS IN JULY

PEOPLE WHO SAY THEY NEED TO GO DURING CHAT, BUT TWENTY MINUTES AFTER YOU SAY GOODBYE, THEY'RE STILL ONLINE

PEOPLE WHO "CHECK IN" AT THE GYM

PEOPLE WHO DECLINE BUTTER ON THEIR POPCORN

O-M-G, PEOPLE WHO USE POPULAR INTERNET ACRONYMS IN EVERYDAY SPEECH (J/K!)

PEOPLE WHO TURN AROUND AND SPEAK TOWARD THEIR POWERPOINT PRESENTATION

PEOPLE WHO ASK YOU TO VISIT THEIR FARMVILLE FARM

PEOPLE WHO THINK THEY CAN GET AWAY WITH TAKING A DUMP WHILE ON THE PHONE

PEOPLE WHO SAY SOMETHING HAPPENED "ALL OF THE SUDDEN"

PEOPLE WHO PUSH ELEVATOR BUTTONS THAT ARE ALREADY LIT UP, JUST IN CASE

PEOPLE WHO ORDER AN APPETIZER AS THEIR ENTRÉE

PEOPLE WHO USE THINGS IN YOUR HOUSE THAT AREN'T ASHTRAYS AS ASHTRAYS

PEOPLE WHO TURN DOWN REAL-LIFE SOCIAL ACTIVITIES BECAUSE THEY'VE MADE COMMITMENTS IN THEIR ONLINE GAME

PEOPLE WHO FRIEND THEIR PROFESSORS

PEOPLE WHO HAVE AN UNDERSCORE IN THEIR EMAIL_ADDRESS

PEOPLE WHO LEAVE THE NEW ROLL OF TOILET PAPER SITTING ON TOP OF THE DISPENSER

PEOPLE WHO WRITE CHRISTMAS CARDS FROM THE PERSPECTIVE OF THEIR PET

PEOPLE WHO SHARE AN EMAIL ADDRESS WITH THEIR SPOUSE

PEOPLE WHO USE THEIR TEETH TO OPEN THINGS

PEOPLE WHO CONTINUE TO SHOW UP AT COLLEGE PARTIES IN THEIR THIRTIES

PEOPLE WHO THINK THEY ARE STILL A VIRGIN BECAUSE THEY DID IT IN THE BUTT

PEOPLE WHO MAKE EXAGGERATED YAWNING NOISES

PEOPLE WHO START DATING ONE OF YOUR PARENTS AND DECIDE THEY WANT TO HAVE A "REAL RELATIONSHIP" WITH YOU

PEOPLE WHO EAT NUTELLA STRAIGHT FROM THE JAR

PEOPLE WHO USE STARBUCKS' CUP-SIZE TERMINOLOGY WHEN THEY'RE NOT IN A STARBUCKS

PEOPLE WHO TRY TO POPULARIZE A NICKNAME THEY CAME UP WITH

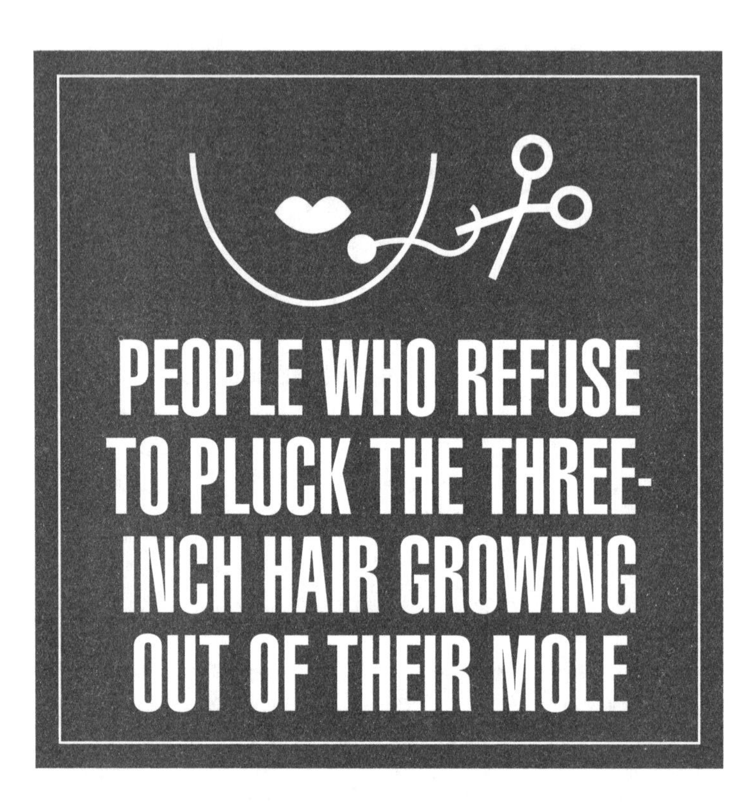

PEOPLE WHO SHAVE THEIR ARMS

PEOPLE WHO KEEP CHUCKLING AT SOMETHING UNTIL YOU ASK THEM WHAT IT IS

PEOPLE WHO, AFTER BURPING, BLOW IT OUT OF THE SIDE OF THEIR MOUTH

PEOPLE WHO POST ENDLESS PHOTOS ON FACEBOOK OF A PARTY THEY DIDN'T INVITE HALF THEIR FRIENDS TO

PEOPLE WHO DON'T DECIDE WHO THEY'LL VOTE FOR UNTIL THEY GET IN THE BOOTH

PEOPLE WHO HAVE EXTENDED LAPSES BETWEEN DYE JOBS

PEOPLE WHO SEND TEXT MESSAGES SO LONG THEY GET BROKEN UP INTO SEVERAL TEXT MESSAGES

PEOPLE WHO ANNOUNCE IT TO THE ROOM WHEN THEY'RE GOING TO PEE

PEOPLE WHO TELL YOU WHAT SORT OF WINE YOU SHOULD BE DRINKING WITH THAT

PEOPLE WHO
CLAIM THEY'D KEEP
WORKING AT THEIR
CURRENT JOB IF THEY
WON THE LOTTERY

PEOPLE WHO BELIEVE
APOSTROPHE'S
ARE THE KEY TO
PLURALIZING NOUN'S

PEOPLE WHO THINK WATCHING A LOT OF SPORTS MAKES THEM SOMEHOW ATHLETIC

PEOPLE WHO ARE CURIOUSLY JUDGMENTAL OF HOW DARK OTHER PEOPLE'S CHOCOLATE IS

PEOPLE WHO, WHILE WORKING OUT, BECOME TRANSFIXED BY THEIR OWN IMAGE IN THE GYM MIRRORS

PEOPLE WHO COME BACK FROM A SEMESTER ABROAD WITH AN "ACCENT"

PEOPLE WHO CAN'T SAY SOMETHING'S IRONIC WITHOUT THEN STARTING TO SING THE ALANIS MORISSETTE SONG

PEOPLE WHO CONSIDER ITALIAN TO BE AN ETHNIC FOOD

PEOPLE WHO TAKE THE ELEVATOR TO THE SECOND FLOOR

PEOPLE WHOSE VOICE GOES UP? AT THE END OF EVERY THOUGHT? SO EVERYTHING THEY SAY SOUNDS LIKE A QUESTION?

PEOPLE WHO SAY ON THE PHONE, "WELL, I'M GOING TO LET YOU GO" WHEN CLEARLY THEY'RE THE ONE WHO WANTS TO BE LET GO

PEOPLE WHO SAY GOODNIGHT TO FACEBOOK

PEOPLE WHO STILL USE THE PREFIX "CYBER-" FOR ANYTHING

PEOPLE WHO JUSTIFY LIVING IN A SHIT-HOLE REGION BY ALWAYS BRINGING UP ITS VERY REASONABLE REAL ESTATE PRICES

PEOPLE WHO LIVE IN A SHIT HOLE THAT'S AN HOUR AWAY FROM THE CITY THEY CLAIM TO LIVE IN WHEN ANYBODY ASKS

PEOPLE WHO TAKE THEIR INFANT TO THE MOVIES

PEOPLE WHO TRAVEL
TO FARAWAY
COUNTRIES AND
INSIST ON EATING AT
THEIR MCDONALD'S

PEOPLE WHO ORDER MENU ITEMS IN A RESTAURANT BY SAYING THEY'LL "DO" THEM

PEOPLE WHO OWN PETS THAT HAVE TO BE FED SMALL, STILL-LIVING MAMMALS

PEOPLE WHO STILL USE "-ALICIOUS" AS A NOVELTY SUFFIX

PEOPLE WHO FINALLY GET TO THE FRONT OF THE LINE AND STILL DON'T KNOW WHAT THEY WANT TO ORDER

PEOPLE WHO CELEBRATE THEIR "ONE-MONTH ANNIVERSARY"

PEOPLE WHO STOP A FULL CAR LENGTH BEFORE THE INTERSECTION

PEOPLE WHO JUDGMENTALLY LOOK OVER YOUR GROCERIES AT THE CHECK-OUT COUNTER

PEOPLE WHO WEAR SHORTS REGARDLESS OF WEATHER CONDITIONS

PEOPLE WHO TEXT YOU WHEN THEY ARRIVE, RATHER THAN RING THE DOORBELL

PEOPLE WHO GO TO THE BEACH AND COMPLAIN ABOUT THE SAND

PEOPLE WHO DECIDE THEY NEED A NEW RINGTONE WHILE RIDING THE SUBWAY

PEOPLE WHO ARRIVE FOR CLASS TEN MINUTES LATE, WITH A COFFEE

PEOPLE WHO, AS YOU'RE WASHING THE DISHES, KEEP BRINGING IN MORE DISHES

Epilogue

A great man (I believe it was me) once said, "Compendia are never finished, only abandoned." Dear reader, such is sadly the case with the volume you now grip between your mammalian extremities. Try as I have to fashion a comprehensive and canonical anthology of all those people who confound us with their persistent existence, I continue to be confounded on a near daily basis. At least, that's what I think is happening; it might just be a side effect of my anti-gout elixir. Alas, all good things must come to an end, and also, books like this one.

What's next for *wireless G*, you ask? I'm heartened by your query, since I was frankly expecting you to inquire about obtaining a refund. Well, a scholar's work is never done! Except over the summer, of course, and for six weeks around the holidays. We are not machines. But in those free moments when I am not consumed by scholarly necessities such as beard-growing and elbow-patching, I will continue my pursuit of the speed record for an unpowered dirigible, which currently stands at forty-three nautical hands per fortnight. Furthermore, I am only five short semesters from receiving my second correspondence doctorate in Applied Phrenology, while my dream of brewing a pure cucumber beer continues to prove elusive. All the while I will, of course, continue to curate the "on-lines" companion to this compendium, which you may dial up on any tube-connected data processing apparatus.

So, let us raise a mug of hooch or alcoholic flu remedy to People Who, and remind ourselves: they know not what they do. For the most part. Often, they may not even know who they are, or how their underwear came to be inside out. They are not just our enemies, but our friends. They are each and every one of us (except me). Therefore, who am I to cast judgment upon such unfortunates? Nay, the purpose of this volume is but to identify and catalog, not to criticize, accuse, or lay blame. That task, dear reader, I leave in your capable hands.